Tamasin Day-Lewis
TOP TARTS
TEN RECIPES

Tamasin Day-Lewis
TOP TARTS
TEN RECIPES

WEIDENFELD & NICOLSON

Tamasin Day-Lewis, a finalist in the *Independent* Cook of the Year competition in 1994, is now widely regarded as one of the great food writers of our time. She writes an avidly followed column for Saturday's *Daily Telegraph* and is a regular contributor to American *Vogue*, *Vanity Fair* and *Country Homes and Interiors*.

After reading English at King's College, Cambridge, she went on to direct many television documentaries for the BBC, ITV and Channel 4.

Tamasin's approach to cookery celebrates comforting, rural recipes, champions seasonal dishes and rekindles the pleasures of 'proper', slow cooking. Her last five books, *West of Ireland Summers: A Cookbook* (1997), *Simply the Best* (2001), *The Art of the Tart* (2000), *Good Tempered Food* (2002) and *Tarts with Tops On* (2003) have all been widely and well reviewed and sold throughout the world. She has recently completed her second 15-part television series, 'Tamasin's Weekends'.

Tamasin lives in Somerset and County Mayo in Ireland.

CONTENTS

When I decided to write a book about tarts, I looked back before I looked forwards. Cooking is always about shared memory and experience, and tarts seem to have both fuelled and inspired my passion for food and cooking for longer than I can remember with any reliable degree of honesty and clarity. I have clear memories of making jam tarts, eating them bubbling hot from the oven and invariably searing one's mouth in a haste to devour them.

The marriage of textures and flavours, colours and aromas, the beauty of turning out the simplest everyday tart, or gilding or glazing one of elegant richness, make tarts the most satisfying of foods to make and eat.

From the classic of tarts, the Quiche Lorraine and the Strawberry Tart, to the airy heights of a Tomato and Prosciutto Tart on a puff pastry base and the ambrosial Peach, Vanilla and Amaretti Tarte Tartin, anyone can bake a tart, and enjoy this most biddable of foods.

'This most versatile and perfectly
self-contained of foods is without
doubt one of the great joys of my
cooking life, equally as pleasurable
in the making as in the eating.'

RECIPES

Serves 6

6 rashers of organic smoked streaky
  bacon
300ml/10fl oz organic double cream,
  Jersey if you can get it
1 organic egg and 3 yolks
black pepper

QUICHE LORRAINE

Make shortcrust pastry (page 36) with 120g/4oz organic white flour
and 60g/2oz unsalted butter, binding the mixture with an egg and a
scant 2–3 tablespoons of water. After chilling, line a 20cm/8 inch
tart tin and prick the base with a fork. Preheat the oven to
200°C/400°F/Gas 6.

Snip the bacon into strips and cook them gently in a frying pan
until the fat begins to run. They should remain pinkly soft, not
crispened. Drain, cool slightly, then spread over the bottom of the
pastry case. Whisk together the cream, egg, yolks and pepper, then
pour into the pastry case and place in the oven for 20 minutes. Turn
the heat down to 180°C/350°F/Gas 4 for a further 10–15 minutes,
until the filling is goldenly puffed up like a soufflé.

Remove from the oven and leave for 10 minutes before serving.
Scalding tarts don't taste of anything.

Serves 6 for supper, 8 for lunch
1 tbsp Dijon mustard
100g/generous 3oz Gruyère, grated
1 dozen or so organic tomatoes, sliced
4 x 125g/4½ oz Camembert-style goats'
   cheeses (I use Soignon, from
   Sainsbury's), sliced

Herbed brushing oil
125ml/4fl oz extra virgin olive oil
1 dsp each of finely chopped rosemary,
   thyme, basil, fennel and flat-leaf parsley
1 clove of garlic, crushed
salt and black pepper
1 bay leaf

TOMATO, GOATS' CAMEMBERT AND HERB TART

Combine all the ingredients for the brushing oil in a jar or bowl and leave overnight if possible, or at least for a couple of hours.

Make shortcrust pastry (page 36) with 180g/6oz organic white flour and 80g/2¾oz unsalted butter, but use your best olive oil instead of water – you might need a bit more than 2 tablespoons. Chill, then roll out and line a 30cm/12 inch tart tin.

Preheat the oven to 190°C/375°F/Gas 5 and put a baking sheet in the oven.

Spread the mustard over the pastry base, then scatter over the Gruyère. Cover with alternate overlapping slices of tomato and goats' cheese in concentric circles, then brush two-thirds of the herby oil over the surface. Bake the tart on the preheated baking sheet for about 35 minutes; it will be heaving, brown and bubbling. Remove from the oven, brush with the remaining oil, and leave to cool for at least 10 minutes before turning out and serving.

A broad bean and asparagus salad would dress it up, a simple green one would dress it down.

Makes 8 small tarts
8 slices of prosciutto, San Daniele
  if possible
150ml/5fl oz best virgin olive oil
3 cloves of garlic

black pepper
10 plum tomatoes, or about
  40 cherry tomatoes
a handful of basil, and the same
  of either thyme or rosemary

TOMATO AND PROSCIUTTO TARTS

Preheat the oven to 190°C/375°F/Gas 5. Start with 300g/10oz of pure butter puff pastry (page 39); this tart is characterized by its buttery, oily flakiness. Roll it out and stamp it into eight 10cm/4 inch circles, then place them on a greased baking sheet and leave them in the fridge until you need them.

Tear the prosciutto roughly and put it in the food processor with half the olive oil, the garlic cloves and the pepper. Blitz for a few seconds to make a rough purée.

Slice the plum tomatoes, or halve if you are using the cherry ones. Tear the basil leaves and add them to the remaining olive oil, but not more than 20 minutes before you are going to use them or they will bruise and blacken.

Spoon a mound of the prosciutto mixture on to each tart base, leaving a good-sized clear edge. Place a circle of tomatoes on top, brush with a little of the oil and basil mixture, sprinkle with roughly chopped thyme or rosemary, and cook for about 15 minutes, until the pastry is puffed up and cooked through. Put the tarts on a rack and brush with the oil and basil mixture, then serve warm.

Serves 6
30g/1oz unsalted butter
1 tbsp olive oil
325g/12oz organic baby spinach

black pepper
200ml/7fl oz double cream
1 egg and 2 egg yolks
12 anchovy fillets

SPINACH AND ANCHOVY TART

Make shortcrust pastry (page 36) with 120g/4oz organic white flour and 60g/2oz unsalted butter, but, instead of adding water, add a generous tablespoon of your best olive oil to the mixture before blitzing it all together. Chill, then roll out and line a 22cm/9 inch tart tin. Preheat the oven to 190°C/375°F/Gas 5. Bake the pastry blind for 15 minutes, then remove the beans, prick the base with a fork, and return to the oven for a further 5 minutes.

While the pastry is in the oven, heat the butter and olive oil in a heavy-bottomed enamel saucepan, add the spinach and pepper, and stir briefly until the spinach has wilted but not lost its shape, about a couple of minutes.

Whisk the cream, egg and yolks together, then pour in any liquid from the spinach pan. Tip the spinach and anchovies into a food processor and process as briefly as you dare, to keep their texture and not reduce them to a slushy purée. Throw them into the bowl with the cream and eggs and stir with a fork, then pour the whole lot into the pastry case and cook for about 25 minutes.

Leave to cool for 10 minutes, then serve with something plain, like a cherry tomato salad, and good, white country bread and butter, as I did for lunch this May Day Saturday.

Serves 6

22cm/9 inch shortcrust pastry case,
  chilled (page 36)
beaten egg, for brushing
325g/12oz undyed smoked haddock
300ml/10fl oz Jersey milk
30g/1oz butter
1 small onion, finely chopped

1 stick of celery, finely chopped
30g/1oz plain flour
salt, black pepper, nutmeg
a bunch of watercress (stalks removed),
  finely chopped
2 eggs, beaten
2 tbsp grated Parmesan

SMOKED HADDOCK
AND WATERCRESS TART

Preheat the oven to 190°C/375°F/Gas 5. Bake the pastry blind for
10 minutes, then remove the beans, prick the base with a fork, and
brush with beaten egg. Return to the oven for a further 5 minutes.

Put the haddock and milk in a saucepan and bring to the boil, then
reduce the heat and simmer for a further 10 minutes. Remove and
skin the fish and flake into a bowl. Reserve the milk separately.

Heat the butter in a saucepan, add the onion and celery and cook
gently until softened. Stir in the flour and cook for a couple of
minutes, then add the reserved poaching milk and stir until the sauce
has thickened. Season with a little salt, pepper and grated nutmeg.
Remove from the heat and stir into the fish, adding the watercress
and beaten eggs. Pour into the pastry case and sprinkle the top with
the grated Parmesan. Bake in the oven for 25–30 minutes, when the
tart will have risen and be crusted a delectable golden brown. Leave
to cool slightly before turning out and eating hot.

Serves 8 greedy people
about 1kg/2lb strawberries
about 4 tbsp redcurrant jelly

Crème pâtissière
375ml/13fl oz Jersey or full fat milk
1 vanilla pod, split
4 egg yolks
120g/4oz caster sugar
50g/just under 2oz cornflour

STRAWBERRY TART

Make a pâte sucrée (page 37) with 180g/6oz white flour, 90g/3oz
unsalted butter, 2 dessertspoons icing sugar, 2 egg yolks and a little
ice-cold water; chill for at least an hour. Preheat the oven to
200°C/400°F/Gas 6. Line a 30cm/12 inch tart tin with the pastry
and bake blind, then remove the beans and return to the oven for
10–15 minutes, until golden and cooked. Watch closely: the edges
burn swiftly, and you don't want scorch marks on the bottom. Leave
to cool.

For the crème pâtissière, scald the milk with the vanilla pod and its
scraped-out seeds. Whisk the egg yolks, sugar and cornflour together
in a bowl, then pour the hot milk on to them and continue whisking.
Remove the vanilla pod. Return the mixture to the saucepan and
stir over a gentle heat until thickened. Turn into a bowl and cool,
whisking every so often. When cold, scrape into the pastry case with
a rubber spatula. Turn the tart out on to a plate or bread board.

Hull the strawberries. Starting at the edge of the tart, stick them
upright into the crème pâtissière in a circle and work your way in,
using smaller strawberries for each circle. Melt the redcurrant jelly
with a tablespoon of water, then brush it liberally over the strawberries
and the custardy gaps. Stand back and admire before you cut it.

Serves 6–8
For the pastry
120g/4oz plain flour
2 tsp Green and Black's organic cocoa powder
1 heaped dsp unrefined icing sugar
60g/2oz cold butter, cut into small pieces
1 egg yolk

For the filling
200ml/7fl oz crème fraîche
250ml/8fl oz double cream
180g/6oz Green and Black's organic white chocolate
200g/7oz fresh raspberries

WHITE CHOCOLATE TART
WITH RASPBERRIES

Preheat the oven to 200°C/400°F/Gas 6. Grease a 22cm/9 inch tart tin.

For the pastry, sift the flour, cocoa and sugar into the bowl of your food processor, add the cold butter and whizz briefly. Add the egg yolk and a tablespoon or two of ice-cold water, and process again just to the point at which the pastry coheres. Wrap in cling film and refrigerate for half an hour. Roll out on some flour sifted with a bit more cocoa and line the tart tin. Bake blind for 20 minutes, then remove the beans and cook for a further 10 minutes. The pastry case should be crisp and browned slightly. Leave to cool.

For the filling, heat the crème fraîche with 100ml/3½ fl oz of the double cream. Break the chocolate into a bowl, pour the hot cream over it and leave for a minute, then stir until the chocolate dissolves. Cover with cling film with some air holes punched in it, and put in the fridge for 2–3 hours.

Very lightly crush the raspberries with a fork, just to let the juice run a little (they should remain whole), and put them in a single layer on the pastry base. Whisk the remaining double cream until thick but still soft, not rigid, and fold it into the chocolate mixture. Smooth this over the raspberry base and refrigerate for at least an hour. Eat cold.

Serves 8
For the pastry
8 amaretti
180g/6oz plain flour, sifted
90g/3oz unsalted butter, cut into pieces
2–3 tbsp iced water

For the top
8 ripe peaches (white are the absolute
best, but yellow-fleshed are fine)
juice of 1 lemon
1 vanilla pod
90g/3oz caster sugar
60g/2oz unsalted butter

PEACH, VANILLA AND
AMARETTI TARTE TATIN

To make the pastry, crush the amaretti in a food processor, add
the flour and butter and process briefly to combine, then add 2–3
tablespoons iced water and process until the mixture comes together.
Wrap in greaseproof paper and chill for at least 20 minutes.

Preheat the oven to 190°C/375°F/Gas 5. Roll out the pastry to
1cm/½ inch more than the circumference of the pan – I use a heavy,
25cm/10 inch diameter frying pan – and set the pastry to one side.

Scald the peaches in boiling water for 30 seconds. Peel, and sprinkle
them with lemon juice to prevent discolouration. Split the vanilla pod
and scrape it out into the sugar. Warm the sugar in the frying pan until
it is a deep, dark brown and totally liquid. Do not stir, but move the
pan around to prevent burning. Remove from the heat and dot with
half of the butter. Put half a peach in the middle of the sugar mixture,
cut side up. Quarter the rest, and, starting at the outside of the pan, lay
them next to each other in a tightly packed wheel. Arrange the remaining quarters in an inside wheel. Dot with the rest of the butter and put
the pan back over the heat for 2–3 minutes to gently start the cooking.

Remove from the heat, cover with a mantle of pastry that you tuck
inside the pan edge, and bake for 25–30 minutes. Remove from the
oven and leave for 10 minutes before inverting on to a plate.

Serves 6–7
22cm/9 inch shortcrust pastry case made
  with wholemeal flour, chilled (page 36)
beaten egg white, for brushing

Butterscotch filling
200g/7oz dark muscovado sugar
250ml/8fl oz single cream

90g/3oz butter
50g/scant 2oz cornflour, sifted
3 egg yolks
1 tsp vanilla extract

Meringue
3 egg whites
60g/2oz caster sugar

BUTTERSCOTCH TART

Preheat the oven to 190°C/375°F/Gas 5. Bake the pastry blind for
15 minutes, then remove the beans, prick the base with a fork, brush
with beaten egg white and return to the oven for 10 minutes. Turn
the heat down to 180°C/350°F/Gas 4.

Put all the ingredients for the filling in the top of a double boiler
and whisk together over a low heat until thick, creamy and lump-free.
Then scrape the filling into the pastry case.

For the meringue, whisk the egg whites until stiff, add one-third of
the caster sugar and whisk again. Add another third of the sugar and
fold it in gently with a metal spoon. Either spread the meringue over
the filling, or mould it into six or seven quenelle-shaped portions
with two large spoons. Sprinkle the remaining sugar over the top and
return to the oven for about 20 minutes, or until beautifully browned
and crunchy on top.

Serves 6–8

½ a large (900g) tin of golden syrup
30g/1oz unsalted butter, cut into
  small cubes
1 large egg, beaten

2–3 tbsp double cream
grated zest of 2 organic lemons
4 heaped tbsp brown breadcrumbs,
  preferably granary

TREACLE TART

Preheat the oven to 190°C/375°F/Gas 5. Make shortcrust pastry (page 36) with 120g/4oz plain or wholemeal flour, or 180g/6oz if you are going to add a lattice top. Line a 22cm/9 inch tart tin and chill. Bake blind for 15 minutes, then remove the beans, prick the base with a fork and bake for 5 more minutes. Turn the heat down to 180°C/350°F/Gas 4.

Warm the syrup gently, then, off the heat, add the butter and stir until melted in. Beat together the egg and cream and add to the syrup, with the lemon zest and breadcrumbs. Stir to mix evenly, then pour into the pastry case, add a lattice top if you like, and bake for 25–30 minutes. The filling will have set to a gel.

Leave for about 20–30 minutes before serving warm – there is nothing like hot treacle tart for taking the roof off your mouth. Dollop on some clotted cream, then go for a brisk artery-defying walk afterwards.

THE BASICS

MASTERING PASTRY

Just as the golden rule for house buying is location, location, location, so for pastry it is cold, cold, cold. Your butter should be chilled, your hands cold, and if you have a morgue-cold marble slab to roll the pastry out on, so much the better. I have even grated butter straight from the freezer when there has been none to be found in the fridge. Warmth and overworking are the enemy to the good, buttery-crisp pastry crust. I make my pastry in a food processor, and stop the button the moment the flour and butter have cohered into a ball, otherwise the results will be a cross between play dough and knicker elastic. Beware, but don't be frightened. Too wet or too dry, it can, like curdled mayonnaise, be rescued.

SHORTCRUST PASTRY

The simplest pastry of all. I use 120g/4oz plain white (preferably organic) or wholemeal flour to 60g/2oz unsalted butter for my 22cm/9 inch tart tin, and 180g/6oz flour to 90g/3oz butter for a 30cm/12 inch tin. Rolled out thinly, these quantities fit perfectly. I would also use the smaller quantity for a 20cm/8 inch tin, in which case there will be a bit left over.

I sift the flour and a pinch of sea salt into the food processor, then cut the cold butter into small pieces on top of it. I process it for about 20–30 seconds, then add ice-cold water through the top, a tablespoon at a time – about 2–2½ should do it – with the machine running. If the paste is still in crumby little bits after a minute or two, add a tablespoon more of water, but remember, the more water you use, the more the pastry will shrink if you bake it blind. One solution is to use a bit of cream or egg yolk instead of water. The moment it has cohered into a single ball, stop, remove it, wrap it in cling film and put it in the fridge for at least 30 minutes.

If you are making pastry by hand, sift the flour into a large bowl with the salt, add the chopped butter, and work as briskly as you can to rub the fat into the flour, with the tips of your fingers only, rather like running grains of hot sand through your fingers. Add the water bit by bit as above; wrap and chill the pastry.

Scatter a bit of flour on your work surface, roll your rolling pin in it, dust the palms of your hands, and start rolling. Always roll away from yourself, turning the pastry as you go, and keep the rolling pin and work surface floured to prevent sticking. Once it is rolled out, slip the rolling pin under the top third of the pastry, and pick it up, judging where to lie it in the greased tin. Again, never stretch it, it will shrink back. Try to leave at least 30 minutes for the unbaked tart case to commune with the inside of your fridge. Or put it in the night before you need it.

BAKING BLIND

If you are baking your pastry case blind, you will need to preheat the oven to 190–200°C/375–400°F/Gas 5–6. Some recipes also tell you to put a baking sheet in the oven to heat up. This can be invaluable if you are using a porcelain or other non-metal tart dish, as the hot baking sheet gives it an initial burst of heat to crisp up the bottom of the pastry. I know that some cooks will be shocked that I could even think of using anything other than metal but, as well as the aesthetic advantage when it comes to serving, china dishes are guaranteed never to discolour the pastry in the way that some metal ones do. If you are using a tart tin with a removable base, placing the tart tin on a baking sheet makes it easier to slide in and out of the oven.

Tear off a piece of greaseproof paper a little larger than the tart tin and place it over the pastry. Cover the paper with a layer of dried beans; the idea is to prevent the pastry from rising up in the oven. When the pastry is nearly cooked (the timing depends on the rest of the recipe), remove the paper and beans and prick the base of the pastry to let out trapped air that would otherwise bubble up. Return the tart to the oven for about 5–10 minutes to dry the pastry base.

GLAZING

Brushing the partly baked pastry case with a light coating of beaten egg or egg white ensures a crisp finished tart.

PÂTE SUCRÉE

This pastry, enriched with egg yolks, is perfect for summer fruit and chocolate tarts. I normally make it like a standard shortcrust, with 120g/4oz flour to 60g/2oz unsalted butter, adding a tablespoon of sifted icing sugar and using 2 egg yolks instead of water. It is even more important to chill this pastry thoroughly.

PÂTE SABLÉE ('SANDY PASTRY')

This pastry is even sweeter, and crumbly, like a buttery biscuit.
I use 180g/6oz flour to 120g/4oz butter, 60g/2oz icing sugar and
2 egg yolks. I put the butter, sugar and egg yolks into the food
processor and work them together quickly, then blend in the sifted
flour and work it into a paste. This needs longer chilling before
rolling out, a minimum of an hour.

PUFF PASTRY

The richest, lightest leaves of buttery pastry, but it does take time, because of the resting time between each working of the dough. I refuse to compromise over the butter question: commercial brands made with inferior fats are just not what puff pastry is all about. I often buy a 1kg/2¼lb sheet of it ready made and rolled from Baker & Spice (46 Walton Street, London SW3 1RB). It costs £16 and is well worth it, for the French flour, Lescure butter and the magic hands of their viennoiserie department.

Sift 180g/6oz plain flour and a pinch of salt into a mixing bowl, then rub in 25g/1oz of butter, as for shortcrust pastry, or use a food processor. Mix in about 150ml/5floz cold water and then gently knead the dough on a floured surface, preferably marble. Wrap it in cling film and refrigerate for 30 minutes.

Take 155g/5oz of butter out to soften, then flatten it into a 3cm/1 inch thick rectangle. On a lightly floured surface, roll out the dough into a rectangle three times the length and 3cm/1 inch wider than the rectangle of butter. Place the butter in the centre of the pastry and then fold over the top and bottom of the pastry to cover the butter. With the rolling pin, press down on the edges to seal in the butter, then give the dough a quarter-turn clockwise. Now roll the dough out so that it returns to its original length. Fold over the ends again, press them together with the rolling pin, and give a further quarter-turn clockwise. Repeat the process once more, then rest the dough in the fridge for at least 30 minutes, remembering which way it is facing.

Repeat the rolling and turning process twice more, then refrigerate for a final 30 minutes before using or freezing. If the pastry gets warm and buttery at any stage during the process, put it in the fridge to chill.

This edition first published in 2004 by Weidenfeld & Nicolson
Recipes first published in 2000 by Weidenfeld & Nicolson
Text © Tamasin Day-Lewis, 2000, 2004
Food photography © David Loftus, 2000, 2004
Design and layout copyright © Weidenfeld & Nicolson, 2004

A CIP catalogue record for this book is available from the British Library

ISBN 0 297 84375 3

Design director David Rowley
Editorial director Susan Haynes
Project Editor Matt Lowing
Designed by Austin Taylor
Printed and bound in Italy by Printer Trento s.r.l.

Weidenfeld & Nicolson
The Orion Publishing Group
Wellington House
125 Strand
London WC2R 0BB